It's GOOD to be ME!

Boosting self-esteem to find your inner hero

written by
Louise Spilsbury

illustrated by
Mike Gordon

Published in 2013
by Wayland

Copyright © Wayland 2013
Illustrations copyright © Mike Gordon 2013

Wayland
338 Euston Road
London NW1 3BH

Wayland Australia
Level 17/207 Kent Street
Sydney, NSW 2000

Editor: Victoria Brooker
Designer: Paul Cherrill for Basement68
Digital colour: Molly Hahn

British Library Cataloguing in
Publication Data
It's good to be me! : raising self-esteem
to find your inner hero.
1. Self-esteem--Juvenile literature.
2. Self-acceptance--Juvenile literature.
158.1-dc23

ISBN: 978 0 7502 7844 7

2 4 6 8 10 9 7 5 3 1

Printed in China

Wayland is a division of Hachette Children's
Books, an Hachette UK company.

www.hachette.co.uk

CONTENTS

What's it all about?

This book is about you. It's about feeling good about who you are. You're special. In fact, there is no one quite like you anywhere in the world! You have your own skills, talents and unique personality.
Feeling good about yourself means knowing the things that make you special and accepting yourself for who you are – inside and out.

▲ It's good to be you! Whether you're short or tall, sporty or studious, hold your head up high and make the most of your talents, skills and ambitions.

What is self-esteem?

Self-esteem is how you feel about yourself and your achievements. When you feel confident and good about yourself, you've got high self-esteem. Having high self-esteem helps you to get the most out of life. When you value yourself and feel worthwhile, you feel happier.

When you care about yourself, you're better at caring about others too, and you make friends more easily. When you believe in yourself, you're willing to take on new challenges and you're more likely to make choices that are right for you. When you respect yourself, other people respect you too.

Building self-esteem

Self-esteem is not something you're born with, it's something you learn as you grow up. Some of your self-esteem comes from stuff other people say or do. Like when a friend thanks you for listening to their problems or when a teacher gives you a good mark. The warm glow you get from positive feedback boosts your self-esteem. But self-esteem is also a skill you can build up like any other – from learning to play a new video game to learning to cook a mean chilli. You just need to put in a little bit of time and effort…

▼ Anyone can improve their self-esteem if they want to, just like you can get better at cooking or at playing video games. You just have to keep working at it.

You can do it!

Start building self-esteem now! Think of one special thing about yourself. It could be something you're good at, like neat writing, or something kind or helpful that you do.

… And that's where this book comes in. Reading this book can help you to feel more confident and positive, to take responsibility for yourself and your feelings, and to get on with other people. It will give you the skills you need to deal with things that bring you down when you should be looking up!

Let's be positive

Being positive is more than just saying 'I'm great.' Being positive is about focusing on what you're good at and the skills you have. One sure-fire way to boost your self-esteem is to know, and make the most of, your good points.

▶ What are you good at?

The one and only

We're all good at different things. What are your strengths? Don't be shy. What are you good at, at home and at school? Some talents are easy to spot, like being good at science experiments or swimming. Other gifts might be harder to see, like being kind and thoughtful or having a head full of wild and wonderful ideas. Don't leave anything out and ask other people what they like or admire about you too. Thinking of specific things you've achieved or that you're good at makes you feel proud.

You can do it!

Make a list of your five favourite skills and talents. Tape this list in a place you'll see it every day, like the wall by your bed. Do at least one of these things every week. Doing something you know you're good at helps to make you feel good about yourself.

▼ You've got the power to shut out negative thoughts. Use it!

Say no to negatives!

Another way to be positive is to say no to negatives. When you hear a negative thought coming into your head, block it. Instead of thinking 'I never win a match', think 'I really enjoy playing tennis.' Instead of thinking 'I've got so much homework to do, think 'If I get on with my homework, I'll finish in time to watch the football on telly.' Or try looking at the benefits of your so-called negative traits. The fact you're a bit touchy may mean you're caring and understanding. The fact you're bossy may make you a good leader.

And if all else fails, remind yourself it's normal to be better at some things than others. OK, maybe you did fail that science test today, but you can feel happy and proud that you're doing well in technology, or another subject that you really like.

Do better at school

Feeling good about yourself can improve your grades at school. It's true! When you believe that you can learn if you really try, you're more likely to do well. Think about a boy, let's call him Zac, who keeps saying to himself: 'I can't do Maths. I just don't get it.' Three things will happen to Zac, as sure as night follows day. 1) He'll start to believe he can't do maths. 2) Because he believes he'll fail, he won't even try. 3) He'll fail!

Work at it

What can we learn from Zac? Well, you can make a difference by saying 'I'll try' instead of 'I can't'. Listen and ask questions. Don't be afraid of looking stupid. If you didn't quite get something, chances are some of your classmates missed it too.

Look at stuff you didn't understand when you get home. Reading it again one step at a time might help you understand it. It also helps to do homework as soon as you get home – falling behind will just make it harder. Do all this and you'll feel good about yourself because you're making an effort.

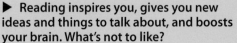

You can do it!

Read and then read some more. Read whatever you like. The sports section in the newspaper, comics, horror stories, online blogs, or cereal packets... Reading boosts your brainpower.

▶ Reading inspires you, gives you new ideas and things to talk about, and boosts your brain. What's not to like?

Find your focus

Knowing the best way you learn helps you to do better at school. If you learn best when listening to music, read through your work at home with your headphones in. If you learn best by talking things through, ask a friend or parent to help you or organise a homework club.

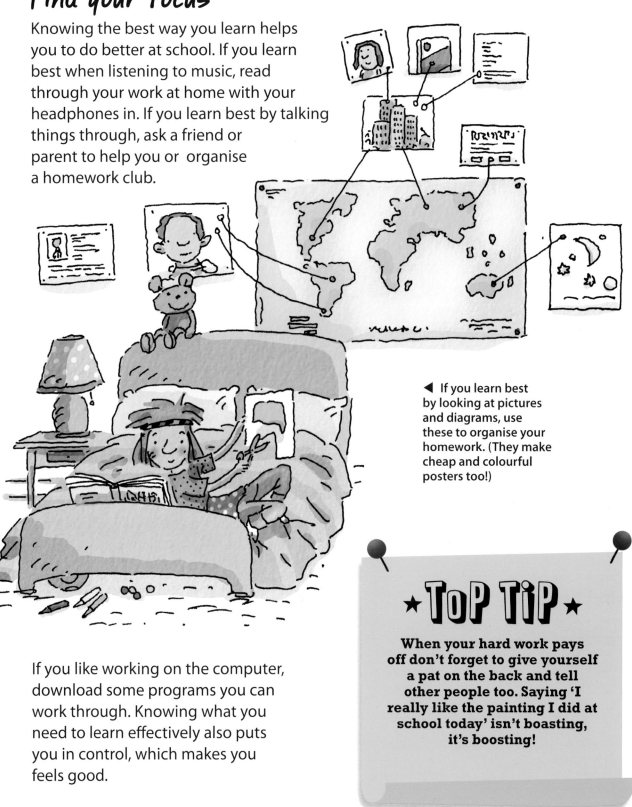

◀ If you learn best by looking at pictures and diagrams, use these to organise your homework. (They make cheap and colourful posters too!)

If you like working on the computer, download some programs you can work through. Knowing what you need to learn effectively also puts you in control, which makes you feels good.

★ **ToP TiP** ★

When your hard work pays off don't forget to give yourself a pat on the back and tell other people too. Saying 'I really like the painting I did at school today' isn't boasting, it's boosting!

Going for goals

How do you feel when your team scores their first goal or you finally learn to juggle three balls at once? Great, huh? When you set yourself a challenge and succeed at it, you feel good about yourself. Don't worry. You don't have to start making plans to climb the nearest mountain – just be willing to have a go at something.

Choosing goals

You can choose a goal to develop one of your hobbies and interests, try something new or aim to achieve something that's important to you. You could plan to keep your room tidy, swim 20 lengths of the pool or improve your spelling. Try to break your challenge down into smaller steps.

▼ Try to avoid goals that simply aren't realistic - like auditioning for a musical if you've got a voice that attracts dogs!

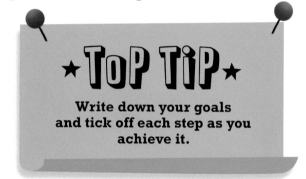

★ TOP TIP ★

Write down your goals and tick off each step as you achieve it.

So, for example, to improve your spelling, you could learn five new words a week and to reach your swimming target you could plan to swim one length further each time you go to the pool.

Changing goals

Don't be afraid to change goals. If you've honestly given something your best shot and can't do it or you decide that it's really not for you after all, choose a different goal. For example, while auditioning for a part in a play, you might realise you'd rather be helping to paint the scenery instead!

Enjoy the ride

Having goals is good, but don't forget that trying to do something can be just as important as actually achieving it.

Enjoy yourself along the way! What if your goal was to become a yellow belt at karate by Christmas and you didn't quite make it? Never mind. By going to karate club all term, you've got fitter, you've had fun and you've made some new friends – that's a great result. Whatever you do, try to make taking part fun – whether or not you win.

You can do it!

When you think of the goal you want to aim for, be specific and be positive. Instead of saying 'I'm not going to sit around after school anymore', say 'I'm going to run around the park for 20 minutes every day after school.' See the difference?

◄ When you've reached one goal, you can always set yourself another. But don't forget to take time off to relax in between too!

Keep at it!

When you're working towards a goal, there will be times when the going gets tough. The task ahead might seem impossible. You might feel like giving up. You might feel plain bored. Hang on in there. If you can keep at it, you'll feel really pleased with yourself, and rightly so.

See into the future

Some sports stars look into the future to motivate themselves, but they don't need a crystal ball to do this! They simply imagine what it will be like to achieve their goal. They watch a movie in their mind of them running fast, winning the race and lifting the trophy above their head. Imagining it helps them to believe it can and will happen and that helps them to get up and go training every morning.

◄ Some people even practise acceptance speeches for their awards long before they reach their goals!

★ TOP TIP ★

Giving yourself a reward when you reach a target on the way to your goal keeps you motivated too. Buy yourself a treat, play a video game, or do whatever else makes you smile.

You can do it!

Make your own mind movies. Close your eyes and think of your goal. Imagine how you'll feel when you succeed and how you'll celebrate. Replay this movie in your head every time you need some motivation.

No excuses

We've all heard some great excuses. How about 'The dog ate my homework', 'A bird snatched it out of my hand', or 'Mum spilt the dinner all over it'? Some excuses are true, but sometimes we use them to avoid doing things. To reach your goals and feel good about yourself, you need to stop making excuses. It's up to you.

Remind yourself why your goal is important to you and why you need to keep at it. Then, next time you find yourself making an excuse, like 'I'd rather watch TV than revise for a test', remind yourself that if you get on with it you can do both. And that you'll enjoy watching TV a lot more when you feel you've done something to deserve it.

▲ If you do your work you won't need excuses like 'The dog ate my homework.'

Make mistakes

No one's perfect. We all make mistakes and we all get things wrong from time to time. Problems are a fact of life and we can't ignore them. The trick is to see mistakes and problems as setbacks, not failures. Don't let them stop you reaching your goals – in fact, mistakes can be a good thing!

▶ Reaching your goal is like a race with hurdles along the track. You have to deal with problems along the way, but you can still reach the end if you keep going!

Jumping hurdles

Making mistakes is one of the ways we learn about the world. Have you seen a toddler learn to walk? They fall down – a lot. They get bumps and bruises, but they also learn something new about walking. Try to do the same when you hit a snag. Pick yourself up, learn from your mistakes and try again. Try to think why you got stuck or why the mistake happened. If you're not sure how to solve the problem, ask other people for ideas. What will you do differently next time?

★ TOP TIP ★

Don't let setbacks stop you. At school one of J. K. Rowling's teachers sat her in 'the dim (stupid) row', but today Rowling is the world-famous author of the Harry Potter stories.

Bounce back

How do you react when someone criticises you about a mistake? Do you take it personally, hang your head and think, 'Yeah, I'm such a loser'? Well, don't. It's normal to feel disappointed when you make a mistake, but just because you messed up on one thing doesn't mean you're a failure.

If you get told off for something, like untidy handwriting or missing a goal, it's best simply to admit your mistake and apologise for it. Don't dwell on it. Just say sorry and move on. Remember, for every one thing you get wrong there will be dozens of other things you get right – you just need to remind yourself of those.

You can do it!

When you have negative thoughts after making a mistake, block them. You could say 'Stop' quietly to yourself or even imagine a referee's whistle blowing in your head. Then replace them with some positive thoughts. Think what you would say to your best friend if they were in your position – and say it to yourself.

▼ Train yourself to bounce back from disappointment! Just because you got something wrong once, doesn't mean you'll always get it wrong.

Like the way you look

When you look in a mirror, what do you see? It's normal to like some things about the way you look and to dislike others, but do you tend to focus on the negatives? To feel good about yourself you need to change how you think about the way you look.

Media-made images

Some people worry about their appearance because they don't think they match up to their 'ideal' body image. For lots of people the ideal body images are those of the models and film stars they see on screen or in magazines. Try not to compare yourself to celebrities. It is unrealistic and unhealthy to try to look like them because their images have been airbrushed or digitally manipulated to make them look different than they do in real life!

▲ The media shows us a very narrow idea of 'beauty'. In reality people come in all ages, shapes, sizes and races.

Eating disorders

It can be very unhealthy to try to achieve a model-thin body. When someone eats too little or makes themselves throw up after eating, in order to lose weight, they have an eating disorder. Eating disorders can make people very ill and stop their body developing properly. Anyone can have an eating disorder – boys, girls, men or women – so if you or someone you know has this problem, see a doctor now.

Accept yourself

How you feel about your body can affect how you feel about yourself. If you worry too much about the way you look, you lose confidence and may miss out on doing things. To get a positive body image, start appreciating your body for what it can do and accept the things you don't like.

Love the skin you're in

One reason to start loving the skin you're in is that there are some things you just can't change, like your shoe size or your height. There's nothing else to do but accept them and think of the upside. So what if you have skinny legs, maybe they're good for running? Most people don't notice the bits that bother you. And even if they do, it probably doesn't matter to them. It's what you're like as a person, not what you look like, that really counts.

You can do it!

When some people imagine the way they look, they see someone shorter, fatter or hairier than they really are. If you have a negative body image, replace it with a positive one. Don't define yourself by something you don't like, such as being too skinny or too short. Focus on something you like – think of yourself as the one with the broad smile or the one with great hair.

▼ If you focus on your good points, other people will do too!

GREAT SMILE

Changing bodies

One reason you're becoming more aware of your body and the way you look is that you may have started or will soon start puberty. This is the part of your life when you grow from a child into an adult and your body changes – a lot. You'll get taller, hairier and spottier and your hands and feet will get bigger. Boys get broader shoulders and girls develop curves. Even your face changes shape a little!

Taking shape

The changes that come with puberty can affect how you feel about yourself. You might become more self-conscious because it feels like you're the only boy in school who's developing body hair or because you're the only girl at school who has to wear a bra.

Some people worry about gaining a bit of weight during puberty. In fact it's normal for this to happen and it's what helps you to develop into your adult shape. Others may feel self-conscious because they are developing more slowly than their classmates.

★ TOP TIP ★

Try to avoid comparing yourself with other people. During puberty everyone changes at different rates. Some people start early and others start later. Most people continue to change until they are 18 years old, so be patient!

▶ You're not alone – most people feel surprised by and self-conscious about the changes to their body during puberty.

You and your body

The shape your adult body eventually takes is mostly down to your genes – coded instructions passed from parents to their children that make us the way we are. Most boys eventually grow to be an average height, although some will always be taller or more muscular than others because of their genes. Some girls will be naturally curvier or skinnier than others, because of their genes. People come in different shapes and sizes – that's just the way it is. There is no ideal shape or size or body type. It's important to accept yourself as you are and as you grow.

▼ Help your friends feel good about themselves by saying something nice about the way they look.

You can do it!

If you are worried about the way you look, try talking to an adult who you trust, like a parent or other family member, a teacher or a coach. They went through puberty too so should be able to reassure you and to give you practical advice, like how to choose a bra or how to shave. If you're very worried about your weight or size, put your mind at ease by seeing a doctor.

Look after yourself

There are lots of things you can't change about your body that you can learn to love or accept. You can also improve your body image by taking care of yourself.

Body care

Taking care of yourself is easy. It helps to get into good grooming habits: take regular showers or baths, clean your teeth so your breath smells fresh, wash and brush your hair and wear clean clothes. It sounds obvious but it really can help you build a positive body image.

◄ It's your body – if you look after it you'll feel better and look better too.

You could also make a plan to eat more healthily and to drink more water. Exercise and healthy eating will help you look good and feel good about yourself. If you want to get fitter, you could make a plan to do some exercise every day.

★ TOP TIP ★

Feeling self-conscious about the way they look stops some people doing exercise. If that's you, why not start off doing dance or fitness DVDs at home or walking until you feel confident enough to join a gym or sports club.

The secret to success

In order to be happy and to succeed in life, your looks and weight don't matter. To make friends, have fun and do well in a career you'll need your personality, talents and other skills. They are just as much a part of you as the skin they come in. It's your hard work that will get you through exams and your kindness and good humour that will win you friends.

You can do it!

Look in the mirror and say three things you like about the way you look and about yourself in general. Ask a friend or someone in your family to do the same. Repeat these things every time you look in a mirror.

Be yourself

The colour of your hair, length of your legs, and size of your waist are not as important as the other things that make you who you are. All you need to do is to make the best of yourself – take care of your body. Then forget how you look and get on with making the most of your life.

▲ How do you want to spend your time? Worrying about the way you look or enjoying life with your friends and family?

21

Take charge of your feelings

Feelings like jealousy, worry, anger and embarrassment are natural and we all have them. The problem is that they can sometimes stop you feeling good about yourself because they can make you feel out of control. It's time to take charge of these feelings!

Deal with it

The first step is to recognise when certain feelings are taking hold. For example, if you're upset because someone seems to have more friends or better clothes than you, say to yourself 'I'm upset because...' or 'I feel jealous when...'. Once you know what your feelings are, you can choose how to deal with them.

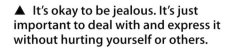

▲ It's okay to be jealous. It's just important to deal with and express it without hurting yourself or others.

Retell the story

Don't beat yourself up about feeling jealous – it's a normal human emotion. But if you often feel jealous about other people, ask yourself if you're reacting to things that are real. For example, a friend sees other people without inviting you and you feel hurt.

If you're low on self-esteem, you may feel like you're losing a friend. Try looking at the situation differently. You're a great friend so it doesn't mean your friend doesn't like you. Maybe they thought you wouldn't enjoy what they were doing, or maybe they just like having other friends too. Seeing things from a positive point of view can make a real difference.

Cut down on comparisons

Feelings of jealousy often come because we compare ourselves to other people. We look at someone else and think they have better clothes than us, a more expensive phone, more friends – the list of possible comparisons is endless. You're even more likely to do this when you're feeling low on self-esteem.

One sure-fire way to reduce jealousy and improve your life is to stop comparing yourself to other people. It's pointless anyway. If you play the comparison game, you'll never win. There will always be people who have more than you and people who have less than you. Try to focus on the things you can do and the things you have, rather than what you don't.

You can do it!

Try this. Instead of comparing yourself to other people, compare yourself to yourself! Think about what you've learned and what progress you've made towards your goals, like learning to skate or passing a test. When you think of all the good things you've achieved, you feel good about yourself without having to think less of other people.

▼ The grass may look greener on the other side, but you never know what's lurking inside it!

Work on your worries

We all worry. People worry when something bad has happened that it might happen again. Or they worry about something happening in the future, like changing schools. Life will always have changes and risks, but you can enjoy the good things and learn to cope with the worries.

Why worry?

Worry can be a useful feeling. It can prepare you for change or for situations you're unfamiliar with. For example, someone who's worried about getting to a new school in case they get lost will try out the route before term starts so that it won't be a problem. Change can be scary but it's also often a chance to learn something new, meet new people and learn new skills – and life would be pretty dull without it. And remember, the more tricky situations you deal with, the more confidence you'll get and the better you'll feel about yourself.

You can do it!

Give yourself a pep talk when you're worried. Say things like 'I've done things like this before' and 'I can stop if I really don't like it'. Remind yourself that you'll be happy with the result or when it's over. Ask yourself questions like 'What's the worst that can happen?' and 'Will anyone even remember this in a month's time?'

◄ It's okay to give yourself a pep talk out loud when you're alone, but when you're out and about it's best to do it in your head!

Relax!

Worry and anxiety often make you feel knotted up inside and make your muscles feel tight and tense. Finding ways to relax your body can also help to relax your mind. Some people use this technique:

Lie in a quiet place and close your eyes. Think about relaxing your body, starting with your feet and legs and then working up to your neck and head, until your whole body is relaxed. Imagine you're somewhere nice and relaxing too, like watching waves lapping on a beach or lying on the grass watching a breeze blow through the trees above. Think about what you can see and how it feels to be there.

Are you relaxed yet?

▲ Relaxation techniques may sound a bit silly, but they really can help people to feel more relaxed – even in stressful situations.

★ TOP TIP ★

Exercise is a great stress-buster. That's because exercise decreases levels of cortisol, a hormone in your body linked to stress, and replaces them with endorphins, hormones that boost your mood.

Act on your anger

Anger itself is not a problem. It can motivate people to get things done, like campaign to save wildlife or report a bully. It's what people do about their anger and how they express it that can cause trouble. You'll feel good if you can control your anger, rather than letting it control you.

▼ Bottling up your anger isn't a great choice. Those feelings might simmer away inside you, making you feel bad, until you explode!

Let it out

It's good to express your feelings. If you bottle up your anger, it just makes you feel bad and possibly even angrier. Instead, say how you're feeling at the time. Remember, your feelings count. If your brother eats your cake, don't blow your top. Say 'I'm angry that you ate my cake.' Or if you're really angry with someone but can't express it, you could write them a letter, email or text saying how you feel. But it's good to wait a day before sending it. When you read it through you might be able to express your feelings more clearly or you may not even have to send it to feel better!

★ ToP TiP ★

It's true - getting a good night's sleep and eating healthy food is good for you. You're more likely to lose your temper when you're tired, and lack of nutrients also makes people feel irritable.

What triggers your anger?

One way to deal with anger is to avoid it. If you can work out what triggers or causes regular angry feelings, you can try to change those things. If you always get angry when your friend makes you late for school, choose to go by bus rather than get a lift with them. Or if a friend always seems to ignore you when she or he is with a certain person, avoid seeing them when they are together. That way you won't have a reason to feel angry.

Keep your cool

If you can feel yourself getting hot and tense and your heart starts pounding because you're getting angry, there are things you can do to calm down. You could try counting slowly backwards, from ten to one, or breathe deeply and slowly for a few minutes. If this doesn't help, walk away from the situation. When you've had time to calm down and think things through, you'll be better able to act on that anger. You can explain what the problem is and what you want to do to resolve it.

You can do it!

Try breathing like this to help calm yourself down: close your mouth and breathe in through the nose deeply and hold your breath for five seconds. Then breathe out slowly through the mouth. Keep going until you feel calmer.

▶ Seeing red? Painting or drawing can be a good outlet for anger. Expressing your frustrations and annoyances on paper can be satisfying.

End your embarrassment

We all feel embarrassed now and then. It usually happens when we've done something we think makes us look silly. It leaves us hot and bothered and sometimes red in the face. Embarrassment can be a pain in the neck if it happens a lot or if it stops you doing things.

Give it a go

People often feel embarrassed when they make a mistake. So, they stay quiet in class and avoid putting their hand up to answer a question, in case they get it wrong. Or they act the fool, pretending they don't care about answering questions anyway. Try to remember it's OK to make mistakes. We all do it. What's important is to keep trying. Why not set yourself a target of putting your hand up to answer at least one question every day or every week. Sometimes you'll get an answer wrong, but sometimes you'll get one right and after a while, you'll forget to feel embarrassed either way.

★ Top Tip ★

Next time you do something that makes you turn a shade of beetroot, remember most people won't even have noticed. If they did they'll probably forget about it in less time than it took you to read this page!

▼ There's no need to go to great lengths to avoid speaking out in class! No one else really notices if you get something wrong. Teachers just want to see people giving it a go.

Ban the blushes

Some people feel embarrassed and blush when attention is suddenly focused on them or when they are not sure how to behave or what to say. This can happen when you don't feel so confident. Maybe you feel embarrassed when someone says something nice to you or about you and everyone looks your way. You deserve compliments and praise too, so try to simply say thank you and smile.

Some people who are easily embarrassed stay in the background and try to avoid social situations. This just makes it worse. It's far better to try to build up your confidence gradually by practising your social skills. The more often you speak up or join in, the more relaxed you'll feel and the less likely you'll be to feel caught out and embarrassed by the things other people say.

▲ Blushing gets worse when you get embarrassed about your embarrassment! When you get tenser, more blood rushes to your face. To cool those cheeks, try to relax, drop your shoulders and breathe calmly.

You can do it!

It can also help to fake confidence in some situations. Hold your head up, smile and look straight at whoever you're speaking to. Pretending you can handle something helps you to get over feelings of embarrassment. And once you've succeeded one time you'll have more confidence the next.

Stand up for yourself

When you're confident and you feel good about yourself, you can stand up for yourself. You know how you feel, you know what you want and what is right for you. You can think for yourself and make decisions for yourself – even when other people are trying to push you in the opposite direction.

Under pressure?

We've all done it. We've all done something just because our friends were doing it. It's natural to want to fit in with people. We all need to feel that we belong. Sometimes friends can press you into doing something that's good for you, like persuading you to join a sports club with them.

But they can also get you to do stuff that is bad for you, like break rules, treat people badly, take risks or start smoking. That's when you need to think for yourself and trust your own judgement. You don't have to believe or do what others say. Just because everybody seems to be

▲ Life is a series of choices. Some are small, like choosing which shirt to put on in the morning. Others are bigger, like whether to bunk off school just because someone you know is doing it. It's up to you to make the right choices!

doing it, doesn't mean it's right. Anyway, most of the time people aren't actually doing half the stuff they say; they're probably just saying it to sound cool.

Say no

When you don't want to do something, the simple answer is to say no. Saying no isn't always easy. You might feel a little left out or worry what people think of you, but you'll also get a warm glow from knowing you did the right thing and stood up for yourself. Some people will respect you for it and some will be glad you said what they were too scared to say themselves. If someone chooses not to be your friend because you won't do it, then they are not true friends. Friends should respect what you want to do and not press you into doing something that makes you feel uncomfortable.

◀ You might find it hard to say 'No' the first time you do it. But standing firm and saying no can boost your self-esteem and give you the confidence to say it more often. Just remember to say yes sometimes too!

★ TOP TIP ★

If you find it hard to stand up to people, get back-up. Talk to a friend to see if they are also unhappy about doing something. Then you can say no together and perhaps even persuade the others to change their minds too!

You can do it!

Practise how to say no before you say it. Choose phrases that sound firm and confident, like, 'I don't smoke because I'm not afraid of saying no' or 'Choosing not to bully someone makes me brave not scared.'

31

Assert yourself

When you have the confidence to say no when you mean no, you're being assertive. Being assertive isn't about trying to get your own way all the time. It's about saying what you think, feel or want in a clear and calm way. It's about having the confidence to express your own opinions.

▼ When you have to assert yourself with someone who's very persistent, stick to what you want to say. They'll get the message – in the end!

Say it again – and again

Some people don't seem to take 'no' for an answer. When you say no, they ask you again. They try to make you feel guilty about letting them down in the hope that you'll say 'yes' instead. You don't have to give in and do something you don't want to do. The trick is to repeat your answer, again and again.

So when your brother says 'Can you do my chores for me? I've got homework to do', and you know he's just making excuses, you could say 'No, I have my own homework to do'. When he says 'Go on, it won't take long' say 'No, I have my own homework to do'. If he says 'Why are you being so mean?' say 'I'm not, I have my own homework to do.' Don't get dragged into an argument or start apologizing. Keep it simple and keep calm until they get it.

Everybody say 'I'

Make a small change in the way you speak to make a big difference in the way you sound. Say 'I' more often! When you tell people what you think or want, you're not telling them what to do or think. You're simply saying that your needs and feelings count. They are as important as everyone else's.

So, instead of saying 'Perhaps we could play cards?' you could say 'I would like to play cards.' Instead of saying 'Maybe we could go to the park?' say 'I want to go to the park. Who'd like to come?' You won't always get your wish, but you will have expressed yourself.

You can do it!

You can assert yourself in arty ways too! Decorate some of your gear so it expresses your personality. Cut out pictures and patterns from old magazines and stick them onto files and folders. You could pick a theme or colour that you like or that says something about you. So, if you play an instrument or want to be in a band, you might choose lots of pictures of groups that you like.

▼ Make your mark on some of your kit. Just check that school and parents are okay about you personalising your kit before you get the glue out.

33

Body talk

The things we say are just one form of communication. You also say a lot about yourself with your body language – the way you stand or sit or make gestures with your hands. When you wave and smile it's obvious you're saying you're pleased to see someone, but what else does your body language say about you?

▶ Which of these two people looks the most relaxed and confident? Why?

Hold it!

The way you hold your body can be a bit of a giveaway. When people are angry they tend to clench their hands into fists or put their hands on their hips. This kind of body language is pretty off-putting! If someone is feeling nervous or a bit shy, they might cross their arms in front of their chest, turn slightly to one side and look down or to the side rather than at the person they're talking to. This body language suggests you want to be left alone. Let your arms relax and fall to the side of your body. Hold your head up and look straight at the person you are speaking to.

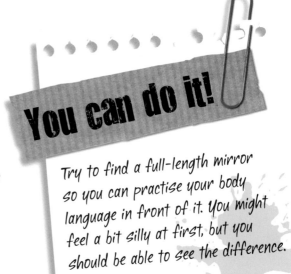

You can do it!

Try to find a full-length mirror so you can practise your body language in front of it. You might feel a bit silly at first, but you should be able to see the difference.

Help yourself

You can use body language to help yourself feel more confident in tricky situations too. Say you have to do something like start a new school or club where you'll meet a whole new group of people. How can you let them know you're a friendly person without even opening your mouth?

To start off with, hold your body in a relaxed, confident way. (Copy the boy in the picture above.) Try to keep your face relaxed too. That means that even if you feel a bit nervous you should try to smile instead of frown or scowl. And when you meet someone, try to look into their eyes and not at the floor when you say hello.

▲ Hold your head up high, walk tall and look people in the eyes and you'll look and feel more confident.

★ToP TiP★

Over half of human communication is through body language and facial expressions. When you're trying to be friendly and confident make sure your body language is saying the same thing!

Coping with conflict

One time it really helps to be able to stand up for yourself is during an argument. It's normal to have rows with friends and family, but you'll be able to sort them out much more quickly if you tackle them in an assertive and positive way.

Argue assertively

When you're upset or angry with someone, try telling them how you feel without blaming them or shouting at them. Otherwise an argument soon gets out of hand. In a calm voice, say 'I don't like it when …' rather than 'You upset me when…' That way you're not blaming the other person, you're telling them how you feel. You could also tell them why something upset you.

▶ When you're upset with someone, say what has happened, how you feel and why. Avoid angry outbursts – they may not even know they have done something to upset you!

For example, if you were cross because a friend told other people one of your secrets, you could say 'I don't like it when you tell my secrets because I don't want other people to know them.' You're not saying your friend's a bad person; just that she did something to upset you. Chances are she'll say sorry and promise not to do it again. What would have happened if you'd have started off by calling her a big mouth?

Talk it out

Most arguments don't get sorted out so quickly because the other person wants to get across their point of view. They deserve to be heard as well. So when you have said what you have to say, pause. Let them speak. Then listen carefully to what they have to say, without interrupting them.

Don't forget to use body language to help things along. Keep your body relaxed and look them in the eyes, so they know you're really listening. That way they'll be more likely to listen to you too, when it's your turn to speak. Talk about the different things you could do to help you both feel OK, until you find something you can agree on.

You can do it!

When you want to talk about something that makes you feel like screaming and shouting, act it out first. Ask a friend to role play it with you. They could play the friend you have a problem with, and you could be yourself, wanting to talk to them about what think is unfair. Ask them to pretend to get cross so you can practise keeping your cool.

▼ Doing a role play of an argument gives you a chance to rehearse things to say that might persuade the other person to understand your point of view in real life.

37

Dealing with difference

What if you have a condition or issue that makes day-to-day life a bit more challenging? For example some people with a learning difficulty like dyslexia or a health condition like epilepsy find that it affects their self-esteem. How can you deal with the extra challenges you have to face?

◄ Knowing about your condition puts you in control. Some people think asthma sufferers should avoid exercise – people with asthma know that a lot of sports are actually very good for them.

Being in control

One thing you can do is to find out all you can about your condition, whatever it is. The more you understand about your condition, the more you can manage it yourself. For example, knowing how to deal with treatments, like anti-epileptic drugs for epilepsy or shots for diabetes, puts you in control.

Being in control makes people feel more confident. And if you understand what causes a learning difficulty and what steps you can follow to deal with it, you'll feel more in control of that too. When we feel in control of a situation we feel stronger and better equipped to deal with other things life throws at us!

Understanding your emotions

It can be quite stressful to deal with all the usual stuff life throws at you – like homework, revision, issues with friends and family – and the realities of dealing with a health condition or learning disorder can add to that stress. So it's important to accept and notice when things get you down or make you frustrated or angry, as that's a natural part of what you're going through.

When you recognise these emotions it can really help to express and share them. Find someone to talk to who you feel comfortable with. It doesn't have to be someone who knows a lot about your condition, just someone who is willing to listen. They don't need to be able to solve your problems, they just need to understand and let you talk things through.

You can do it!

Many people living with serious or chronic illnesses such as cancer find that it helps to have several different people they can talk to at different times, like a therapist or support group specifically for people with their condition as well a close friend or family member they can confide in. There may be support networks at your school or nearby or you may be able to join an online support group.

▲ Support groups are places where people who have the same problem talk about their feelings and offer advice.

Dealing with people

Most of us want to fit in so it can be hard to feel different around friends and classmates. That means some people with a condition or difficulty try to keep it secret. There is no reason to feel embarrassed. Having a health condition or a learning difficulty is not your fault, and a lot of other people face challenges like these, too.

To tell or not to tell?

You don't have to tell people about your condition. That's your choice. Some people are very private and don't want everyone to know. They may prefer to tell only their close friends, and that's okay. But talking to friends and being open about your condition can stop people making silly comments and can help to avoid misunderstandings that can make life harder. For example, someone who has to miss school for treatment might be teased for skiving if classmates don't know why.

▲ Don't be bullied or picked on. Tell a teacher and your parents if somebody is bothering you about your condition, or anything else.

Or someone who has Attention Deficit Disorder (ADD) may be teased for not being clever or trying hard enough. In fact, ADD causes subtle differences in the way a person's brain works, making it hard for them to sit still and concentrate for example.

How to talk about it

If you decide to tell classmates about your health condition, it can sometimes help to remind them that everyone is made differently. Just like some of them have brown hair and others have black hair, some people have certain conditions while others don't.

Most people find that when they talk openly about their condition, others are very understanding and interested and often openly admiring about the things they have done and have had to deal with. Some friends may even offer to help, so you might also want to think of ways others could help so you can ask them for what you'd like – even if it is that they all stop asking questions and just treat you normally!

▲ When people explain their condition to classmates, they are often surprised at how accepting and understanding most people are.

You can do it!

Do you have to do something in front of classmates that makes you feel a bit embarrassed, like give yourself a shot of insulin if you have diabetes? Some people find that it helps to talk to their class about what's going on. If you or your teacher explains it to people, everyone will understand what you're doing and why.

The real you

Some people feel like the difficulties in their life are what defines them. It's easy for a health condition or learning difficulty to become the main focus of your life in the early stages when you're just learning about and starting to deal with it. But it's important to remember that it's just one small aspect of the real you.

Keep things in perspective

Sometimes people let problems in one area of their life spill over to others. For example, someone with learning difficulties may start to think of themselves as stupid or slow at everything just because they face challenges with aspects of school work. In fact, the opposite is usually the case.

Most people say that they learn more about themselves through dealing with their particular challenge and that they grow to be stronger, more determined and more self-aware than they would if they'd never faced it.

▲ Your condition is just one part of you. What are the many things that make you who you are?

★ TOP TIP ★

You can aim high! Keira Knightley and Orlando Bloom struggled with dyslexia in childhood but both became award-winning actors, and Steve Redgrave, who has diabetes, won five Olympic gold medals for rowing.

It's good to be different

The best way to feel good about yourself is to recognise and appreciate the things you are good at. That means reminding yourself what makes you different in a positive light. If you have learning difficulties think about what your strengths are in non-academic areas like music, art or sport.

◀ Instead of spending time worrying about what you can't do, why not spend time perfecting and doing the things you can!

You can do it!

Helping others and giving back to the community can give you a new perspective on things and help you to feel good about yourself. When we help someone in need it can make our own troubles seem easier to manage. For example, you could help out with younger children who are having difficulty reading or volunteer at an animal rescue centre.

Think about the positive traits in your personality too, like kindness, helpfulness or your ability to make people laugh. Make a list of any progress you make and keep adding to it, because this will encourage you to keep going when you have a bad day. It's also vital to keep seeing your friends and making time for your favourite hobbies and activities out of school.

Friends and first love

Everybody needs friends. Friends help you to enjoy the good times and get through the bad times. When other people believe in you, you feel you can take on the world, but when you have problems with friends, it can drag you down.

◀ Friends can help to spur us on to greater things!

What makes a good friend?

A good friend is someone you have fun with, who is happy for you when you do well and who you feel safe talking to about feelings and problems. They keep your secrets and care about what you have to say and what you want to do.

They say sorry if they upset you or make a mistake. Some people have one or two best friends, but it's good to have other friends to share different interests with, at school, in your street and in clubs.

Making friends

If you move schools, a friend leaves the area or you just want a new friend, how do you go about it? The best way to get to know new people (and have fun) is to join a club, sports or after school activity that you're interested in. Look out for people who have similar interests or sense of humour to you, even if they look or seem different at first.

Think of some things you could ask them, such as what sports, music or games they like. Listen carefully to their answers so they feel like you're interested in what they're saying and follow up with other questions. You could even learn a few jokes – they make great icebreakers. Don't give up trying to make new friends if you're unlucky at first.

★ TOP TIP ★

Remember to use your positive body language. Show people you're interested by standing with your body facing towards them, smile and look them in the eyes when they look at you.

If someone doesn't like you don't worry – you can't expect everyone to like you. After all, you don't like everyone either, do you? Just keep trying.

▼ When you join a club and do an activity with new people, you often find that you make friends without even trying.

Breaking friends

Good friends boost you up, but bad friends bring you down. Sometimes friends grow apart, but sometimes you might need to end a friendship. So how do you know when a friend is no good for you and when you should end a friendship?

What makes a bad friend?

Does a friend make you feel bad often? Look at the questions below. If they do things like this a lot of the time, you need to ask yourself if they really are your friend.

• Do they say mean things like 'You're so bad at Maths, you must be stupid.'
• Are they sarcastic or mean to you often?
• Do they tell other people your secrets?
• Do they bully you or boss you around?
• Do they act like your ideas and feelings aren't important?
• Do they make you do things you don't want to?
• Do they try to stop you having other friends?

▲ We all make mistakes and even best friends argue sometimes and let each other down. If you usually like a person, even a bad row doesn't mean that they are a bad friend.

★ TOP TIP ★

Just because someone argues with you or upsets you, doesn't make them a bad friend. Lots of friends fight now and then. Just make sure you can talk things over, then a few squabbles shouldn't spoil a friendship.

How to break a bad friendship

It's hard to break friends with someone. Most of us do our best to forgive people and to avoid hurting other people's feelings. But you don't have to stay friends with someone who is a really bad friend. You could try letting them down gently. If you say something like 'I'm sorry, I'm busy after school and don't have time to go to the park this week' politely every time they ask to see you, they should get the message. Although it's often quicker and kinder to be straightforward and to say something like 'I'm sorry, but after you told everyone I'm scared of spiders I can't trust you and I can't be friends with someone I can't trust'.

▼ Ending a friendship is a big deal. So make sure it's the right thing to do, and think about offering someone a second chance if they ask for one or deserve it.

You can do it!

When you break friends with someone, plan what to say so you can do it as firmly but kindly as possible. Try to put yourself in their place and think how you'd feel. Be honest but keep it short and simple and don't be rude. You could even role play it with someone else before you do it, so you're fully prepared. Try to keep your cool.

Beat bullying

Bad friends and bullies are bad for you. When bullies do things like insult, push, hit, threaten, or leave someone out time and again, it's damaging. As well as causing pain, bullying knocks your confidence. Some people even start to think the bullies are right and there is something wrong with them. There isn't and dealing with bullying can help you feel good about yourself again.

What's the difference?

There's no logic to who bullies choose to bully, although often they go for someone who is a little different in some way, like a vegetarian in a class of meat-eaters, or someone who's clever or new. Bullies aren't very imaginative! Some people try to stop bullies by changing themselves, like dropping grades if they've been called a swot. It rarely works. Don't stop being you. No one's happy if they can't be themselves. It's the bullies who have to change, not you. To make them change you need to stand up for yourself.

You can do it!

Try writing down what happens every day in a diary. You can write things that happened and how you feel. You can be totally honest because a diary is just for you. No one else sees it unless you want them to. It's a good way to get things off your chest and it'll help you remember when and how things happened when you tell someone about the bullying.

◀ Writing a diary is a good way to let off steam and putting worries down on paper makes a lot of people feel better.

Stand up for yourself

Standing up for yourself against bullying does not mean fighting or shouting back. That won't help – it usually causes more trouble. When bullying starts, there is only one course of action. Keep a record of what happens, such as copies of things like abusive texts, and tell someone. Tell a friend, parent, relative, teacher, head teacher or school counsellor.

If you show the bully you're not afraid to talk about it and won't keep it a secret it shows you're not prepared to let them continue. They may get off with a warning if they say they were only teasing, but chances are they won't do it again because they know that if they do you will not take it lying down.

▲ A bully thrives on secrecy. Take that away and it's like taking the air out of a balloon – they'll soon be deflated!

★ TOP TIP ★

Some people worry what will happen when they tell someone about bullying. You can choose what you would like to happen and talk about it. Maybe you could go to school by car rather than going on the bus for a while. Or maybe you want everyone to know, to show the bullies you won't put up with it.

First love

What if you want to be more than friends with one of your classmates, or someone else you know? You know you feel differently about them because when you see or talk to them your face gets hot and your heart races. You've got a crush – and that can be exciting and confusing!

Coping with a crush

These feelings may be new to you and they can be pretty intense. Lots of people feel a bit awkward at first and unsure what to do. Talking to friends can help, although lots of people like to keep their feelings private at school.

If you do talk about someone you like, choose a friend you can really trust. Otherwise you may end up feeling embarrassed or angry if they tell people and classmates tease you about your crush.

▼ If you need advice or help about a crush, try talking to a parent or trusted adult. Remember, they probably felt the same when they were young too!

What next?

Some people are happy just enjoying the buzz they get when they see their crush, but what if you want to tell them? First, try to work out if they like you back. Suggest doing something in a group with other friends too, to see how you get along. Are they giving you any signals they like you too, like always talking to you or sitting next to you?

If you say that you like someone and find out they only like you as a friend, don't let it knock your confidence. You may feel a little hurt, but you were brave enough to give it a try and that's great. There'll be someone else out there. Just as we have different friends in our lives, everyone has different crushes too.

You can do it!

What do you do if someone has a crush on you but you don't feel the same? If someone says they like you, but you don't like them, try to tell them in a kind way. Some people get embarrassed and stop talking to the person, but try not to do this. Just explain that you're not ready for a relationship like that, but you'd still like to be friends.

▲ Being told 'no' can feel bad. Reduce the chances of it happening by working out whether someone likes you first. What signals are they giving you?

Heartbreak

Few first loves last. That's a fact. So if you break up with someone, you're not alone. It happens to everyone – just think of all the people who have written songs about it! When it happens you might be left feeling sad, disappointed and rejected. What can you do to recover?

Focus on you

The first thing to remember is that just because one person doesn't love you, doesn't mean you are unlovable. If someone doesn't feel the same as you, it's better to know now than later when it might hurt even more.

▼ If your feelings get hurt, don't give up on love! Most people have several crushes before they find someone they really connect with.

If someone says something mean when they break up with you, try to remember that your value as a person doesn't depend on what other people think. Trust yourself. So if someone says you wouldn't let them have any other friends and you know that's true, well it's not a big deal, just something you may want to work on. If you know what they say is not true, forget about it. Either way, you're OK.

You can do it!

Remind yourself what is great about you. Make a list of all the reasons your friends and family love you and stick it by your mirror. Remind yourself you're special and that you just need to wait a bit longer to meet someone who appreciates all the good things about you.

Talk about it

Some people find that talking through their feelings with an older brother or sister or someone else they trust really helps. It can help to hear other people's stories of their heartbreak, as it reminds you that you will get over it at some point and that you will meet other people that you like one day.

Sometimes you might just want a shoulder to cry on. If that's the case, you could tell your friend or relative that you'd really like it if they could just listen to you so you can let your feelings out.

★ ToP TiP ★

It's good to spend some quiet time in your room, but don't overdo it. Spend some time with friends, doing things you like or perhaps try something new. Make plans to do lots of things that make you feel good.

▲ Sometimes it's good to listen to sad songs and have a good cry, but you can also use music to cheer yourself up. Why not blast out a classic dance track and sing and bop your way out of the blues?

Talking to adults

Dealing with parents, teachers and other adults can be tricky, especially if you're not overly confident. But you have opinions and you have the right to be heard, so here are some tips to make it easier.

★ToP TiP★

You might feel that your parents don't understand you. Remember they were young once so they should understand if you explain how you feel. Things will get easier over time if you both keep talking.

Getting adults to listen

When talking to an adult, perhaps discussing a problem with a teacher for example, these tactics can help.

- Try not to speak in an angry or whiny voice. Being friendly and respectful will help people hear what you have to say and encourage them to speak to you in the same way.
- Explain yourself clearly and directly. Keep things simple and only say the stuff that's important. The listener is more likely to understand or help if you say what's really going on.
- When you're talking about an issue at school, don't make it personal. If a school rule makes you cross, explain why but don't take your anger out on the teacher. Listen to their answers and reasons.

◀ Some adults are relaxed and easy to talk to, but others can be much harder to deal with. The tips on this page can help give you the confidence to approach them.

◀ There are no guarantees an adult will agree with your opinions, but the way you speak to them can influence how well they listen to and understand you.

Accepting outcomes

Even when you explain yourself clearly and respectfully, an adult won't necessarily agree with you. For example, even if you have good reasons for needing another week to finish an essay, your teacher might not grant it. Adults should listen and take your point of view into account, but they may still say no.

That might not be the answer you want to hear, but it's important to react to their response in a mature way. You can say you're disappointed and that you hope they might reconsider, but try not to get angry about it. Accepting decisions politely will win you more respect and show the adult you are mature. That makes it more likely they'll listen to you sympathetically in future.

You can do it!

Sometimes, however well you explain what you need to an adult, they cannot help you. It may be that a parent has problems of their own and just can't be there for you at that moment or perhaps you think a teacher is being unfair or overly negative. If you can't talk to one adult, find and talk to other adults you can trust. Find a relative, coach or counsellor who will listen and understand, and help you.

Tough talking

What if you have to tell your parents some important or bad news, like explaining why your school report was bad, or if you need to talk to them about something embarrassing or something that's worrying you? Finding the right way to talk to parents can be even tougher at times like these.

Explain how you feel

You could start by telling a parent that you're feeling nervous or worried about discussing something. It may make them a little concerned about what you have to say, but it should also prepare them to be more understanding. For example, if you're worried that they'll be disappointed in you because you've failed a test, say so. They will probably be more sympathetic when they know you care what they think. If you explain that you're embarrassed about asking something personal, they'll probably try to make you feel more comfortable about it.

You can do it!

Pick the timing of a tricky conversation carefully. While you're driving in the car or walking the dog together can be a good time, but not when a parent is really stuck into something else. If they're busy, ask when they'll be free for a chat and pick a quiet, private place to talk in.

▶ Talking to a parent while you're in the car is a good tactic, so long as your mum isn't a rally driver!

Think before you speak

It also really helps to think about what you're going to say before you say it. A bit of forward planning can help you to explain what the problem is in the best possible way. It also means you can think ahead to what your parent's response might be, so you can think of some answers beforehand. For example, if you have to tell them you broke a valuable ornament and you know they'll be mad, you can plan ahead to think of a way you could help them to pay for a replacement.

Be clear what you want

Planning ahead also gives you a chance to think about the kind of response or advice you hope to get from your parent. For example, if you just want to be able to tell them something without them commenting on it, say so. If you want their advice about a tricky situation, be clear about that from the start. If you're in trouble and you'd like them to help you sort it out without giving you a lecture first, explain why.

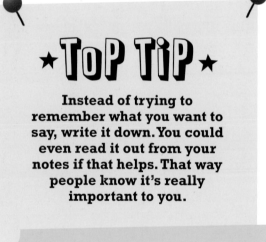

★ Top Tip ★

Instead of trying to remember what you want to say, write it down. You could even read it out from your notes if that helps. That way people know it's really important to you.

◄ Parents aren't mind-readers! If you tell them how they can help, you are much more likely to get what you need from them.

Fighting with families

As you're getting older you probably want to make more of your own choices and decisions, and this can cause disagreements with your parents. That's normal, but for the sake of family harmony and to feel good yourself it's best to keep rows to a minimum.

Chatting is good

One way to keep parents sweet is to chat to them, every day. You don't have to talk for long or about a lot, but spending some time together talking to them about everyday stuff will make you all feel closer. Talk about anything, from big school news to what you had for lunch. The fact that you're used to chatting together will make conversations run more smoothly when you do argue, and it'll probably mean both you and they are prepared to forgive and forget more quickly afterwards.

You can do it!

Chatting to parents about your day-to-day life should stop them asking you a lot of questions (which can be a bit annoying). As well as you telling them about yourself, why not go one better and ask them about their day and their feelings too!

▲ Try to be polite, helpful and considerate toward parents, relatives, teachers, and other adults in everyday life. Being on good terms with adults generally makes it much easier to talk to them when you need to.

Work it out

When you do have a disagreement with your parents or anyone else in your family, try to remember these useful nuggets of advice:

- *Keep calm. Even if you're hopping mad, don't shout and scream or hurl abuse. If you need to, use some calming techniques before you talk or take out your anger by punching a pillow or going for a walk. Then talk calmly and clearly.*
- *When they speak, try to see things from your parents' point of view too. If you can tell them you understand what their problem is, they will try to see things from your side too.*
- *If you can't persuade them to give in, go for a compromise. That's when you come to an agreement that everyone is OK with. For example, you could agree to do your homework straight after school every day for a week if they let you stay at your friend's house on the Friday night.*

▲ It's important to remember that parents don't make rules to make you miserable, it's just that they love you and want to protect you and keep you safe. Some can take it too far…

★ Top Tip ★

Always tell your parents the truth. If you do, your parents will trust you more. If you sometimes lie, your parents may stop trusting you. Then they will be less likely to let you make your own decisions.

You're worth it!

It takes a bit of time to learn anything new, whether it's spelling or surfing. And it takes time for a new habit to become so much a part of your life that you do it without thinking, like getting up early for school every day after a long summer holiday!

That's because your brain needs time to get used to new ideas, until something becomes so familiar it's just part of your routine. It's the same with self-esteem. Work on some of the suggestions in this book as and when you need them, and gradually you'll feel your confidence growing. Soon, you won't just feel good about yourself, you'll feel great!

You can do it!

To feel good about yourself, you need to take good care of yourself. Try to eat healthy food most days, get the sleep you need at night and get regular exercise. Do things you enjoy. Ride your bike, dance, bounce on a trampoline, play tennis, football or go rollerblading. Reward yourself when something you do goes well. Be good to yourself and you'll feel good about yourself.

Practise your positives

Remember, the way you see and interpret things matters. Life isn't perfect and problems are a part of everyday life, but you can train yourself to deal with them better. If someone is rude to you, instead of thinking that nobody likes you, think maybe that person is having a bad day. If you miss the bus to school, don't panic and get down about it, sort it out and get on with the rest of your day. Practise your positives until they come naturally to you.

▼ Building up your confidence takes effort but you will get it. Just give it time!

Taking it further

What if your self-esteem is really low and you're facing serious problems – like a death in the family or your parents are divorcing – that make it really hard for you to improve your self-esteem? In some cases, it can help to see someone who is trained to help with problems like these, such as a counsellor or therapist.

These experts can help you through rough or tricky times. To get the number of someone like this you or your family could call your school or local health centre for a contact number for the appropriate specialist. Lots of people see specialists like this for help. It's just like seeing a doctor about a sore leg or a mechanic about a problem with a car. Sometimes everyone needs a little extra help to make things better.

▲ There's no need to bottle things up. There are lots of people out there who can help to make you feel good about yourself. You're worth it, and never forget that! Altogether now: 'IT'S GOOD TO BE ME!'

Your rights

We all have certain rights. Here are a few of them. It is your right:
• to have your opinions respected
• to have your best interests considered at all times
• to be given the chance to learn effectively and develop as a person
• to live without fear and to feel safe
• to be different, special and unique…

Test yourself!

Try this quiz to find out how you're doing in the self-esteem stakes. Do you make the best of yourself or do you need a self-esteem boost?

1 Do you think someone with self-esteem...
  a thinks they are great
  b thinks they are better than other people
  c knows their good and bad points and is happy with the way they are?

2 What happens when you have a negative thought about yourself?
  a Bad thoughts multiply until you start to think you're useless at everything.
  b You try to stop it but you can't help dwelling on it.
  c You block the bad thought and put a positive slant on it instead.

3 What do you do when you're struggling with a school subject?
  a Think 'I'll never get this' and switch off for the rest of the lesson.
  b Read through the work at home to see if you can get it but then give up.
  c Work on it with a parent or friend and ask the teacher for help. You won't give up!

4 How do you handle mistakes or setbacks?
  a You feel like a failure and get totally knocked back by it.
  b You feel upset but try not to think about it.
  c You try to learn from your mistake and move on from it.

5 What do you think when you look in a mirror?
  a Nothing - you try not to look in a mirror because you don't like what you see.
  b You try to be positive but you can't help dwelling on your bad points.
  c You focus on your good points and accept the rest – you've got more interesting things to think about anyway!

6 Your best friend has a film night with some other mates. Do you…
  a feel jealous, left out and convinced they don't like you anymore
  b accept it but wonder if they are having doubts about your friendship
  c feel fine – it's normal for you both to want to see other friends too?

7 What do you do if someone makes you angry?
  a Bottle up your feelings inside until you feel really hurt and even angrier
  b Let your feelings out by shouting and screaming so you still feel upset after
  c Count to ten and calmly explain what the person has done to upset you.

8 When you walk into a room full of strangers, do you…
  a go straight to a corner and turn away from the crowd
  b stand near people but cross your arms and look down
  c hold your head up high, smile and look people in the eyes?

9 A friend wants you to skip school for the afternoon with them. Do you…
  a say yes – you always go along with other people even if you don't want to
  b say no a few times but then give in under pressure.
  c keep saying no, explain why and persuade them not to do it either?

10 You join a new club, but after a few weeks it isn't working out. Do you…
  a stop going and feel like a total failure, as per usual?
  b keep going and try to make a go of it?
  c choose another club but look on the positives you got from the other one - you may not have learned to line-dance, but you got fitter along the way!

11 When someone you like rejects you, do you…
  a think no one will ever like you again
  b try to be positive but spend a lot of time wondering what you did wrong
  c see your friends and make plans to do things that make you feel better?

Answers

Mostly As… - You've got so much going for you but you don't know it yet! Try out some of the suggestions in the book and soon you'll feel as good about yourself as you should do!

Mostly Bs… You're getting there. You know what you need to do to improve your self-esteem, you just need to work on it a bit more. You know you're worth it – you just need to hone those skills!

Mostly Cs… You've got it! You've got a positive attitude and a firm self-belief that will help you to deal with whatever life throws at you.